Recipe
For
A
Mountain

This book was printed with poison ink.
But you probably won't die from reading it.

For Breanna,
swirling through the world
with magnetic hands.

FOREWORD

Some legends are born into the lap of luxury, known and understood from birth to death. Others are puked out into stale and secluded grottoes, only to surface years down the line as golden children of the fortune five hundred. Well, the sweet spirit that wrote this here book is a scholar of beauty marks; a poet of orgasmic proportions; a bard and a barker of years yet to come; a prostitute to his own creative soul; a millionaire of metaphor; and a sonofabitching orator of the present moment: he's a goddamn legend, and nobody knows it.

The whereabouts of Shimmy Boyle are hazy at best, but at least let me give you this:

After six months of sea travel, running spices from port to port in South East Asia, most men get a little restless. I had settled in a small kampong in the Malay Peninsula. What little money I had was funneled into a store of convenience, which wound up being a lucrative business of slinging contraceptives to the islanders. Sure it was a tough sell, not many people trust a man named Norris, but I worked the locals with sincerity. At first, I'd throw a condom in for free, just dropping a line about how it saved the egg from another infiltration, blah blah. In any event, in a month or so, I had the whole island (male and female) coming through and cleaning me out of all the rubbers, sheep skins, and ziplock bags I had--it was one safely saran-wrapped love-out. But I digress, the poet at hand didn't actually cross my path until a month after all this, I just thought you should know what kind of perspective you're receiving.

I left the Maylay Peninsula in favor of Bangkok; once the condoms ran out, the locals got a little tired of this old sack sitting around puffing smoke up their rears, and when I started getting the hard stares, I knew it was time to leave. In Bangkok, I hooked myself in with Python Manny, a local fight promoter and hostel operator. As I recall, I was working the night shift at the front desk of the hostel when I first met Lt. Shimmy S. Boyle. He traipsed into the dimly lit corridor reeking of saltwater and stale croutons. I had spent the last few hours sharing a hash pipe with Chet the janitor, and my mood was foul, but even through the fog of my stupor I could tell that something strange was brewing. From the end of the hall, all I could make out was the fantastic beard the Lieutenant was sporting. I have found that you can tell a lot about a man based on the caliber of his facial hair, and judging by the demented baby porcupine living on his jaw, Shimmy Boyle was a man to be trusted and respected. He sauntered up to the counter, tossed out 42 bahts, and coughed something about needing a room with a view of the foyer. In my hash haze I took his money, kicked him the key, and shut the lights out.

6 a.m. has always been a time of day that speaks to me in strange ways. 6 a.m. is like the call from the casual lover you impregnated: it is loud, unexpected, and never what you wanted. I awoke to the Lieutenant standing over me brandishing a large bottle of Glen Livit single malt scotch. "You want a kiss from the gods?" he barked in his lamb's breath falsetto. I had been pussyfooting around with the rice wine for several months now, and was in no real condition to accept such an offer, but "When In Rome..." as they say, or Bangkok as it were. It was at this early morning nightcap that Shimmy divulged the following manuscript to me, and essentially changed my life entirely. I remember him sheepishly asking if I would care to look at what he was working on. Shimmy left me the book, and traipsed off to finish the bottle with his morning shower.

You see what I know now is that Shimmy Boyle is a vagabond of renowned proportions and he has made his living cataloguing life with the supple vocabulary he was born with. I rifled the pages with an intense curiosity: Who was this man? What were these words? Why was he doing this? What the hell was in that whiskey?

I finished the book right at 8:30 a.m. I remember because the breakfast bell rang. I stumbled to Shimmy's room, but he was gone. On his night stand sat an index card folded in half. On the outside was a smiley face sitting over two crashing waves and a solitary redwood tree. On the inside of the card was one word: proliferate. My head swam. I was pretty sure he had stolen my wallet.

And so it is that I submit to you the following musings as a testament to the proliferation of life. Open your mind and drink. Open your heart and breathe. It isn't about these particular words, and it isn't about the man who wrote them. It is about the fact that right now has always been the time to start living. So live. This is the moment you have longed for. This is the moment the myth is birthed within us all.

And if you see Shimmy, give him a firm handshake and a hard sock in the jaw. Tell him Norris sent you. Tell him he still owes me that 40 bucks. And tell him if he ever makes a move on my sister again, I will sonofabitching kill him.

Norris H. Buckman
June 12, 2009
Studio City, Ca

PROLOGUE

I bound my body to this book,
gave it my voice and the strength to speak,
so that I may come apart
and learn to wear the sea
as a garment inside my chest.

1

In Search Of Everywhere

The Trees Haven't Yet Figured Out Why
We Get Lonely

The trash man sleeps on a bed of burning candles.
He keeps moonlight in his pocket,
And when he dreams it sings to him.
His teeth are peach pits.
His collar bone, an aluminum can.
He wears his halo in his smile.
In the middle of the night, from beneath the freeway,
He listens to the motorcycles whine.
And if it is late enough
They sound to him like bed sheets
Turning beneath a lover's back
As she rolls toward him,
An ocean of softness
Wanting to touch him
Even in her sleep.

The Opposite of Home

I am standing motionless
In the chattering teeth of morning,
Holding out two hands filled with emptiness,
Making wishes like friends,
Watching the sun spread across the sky like a smile.

In my bloodstream
Are trapdoors to the tops of trees.

I would give both my wrists
To the moon
If it would teach me to sing songs
Made of water.

Honey Raincoat
-For Dustin Wright

It is a soft croon, the way he sings it.

It enters you like an ache,
Fills you with pollen,
Teaches you to stand like a flower,
And buzzes the honeybees around you.

The music is like surgery,
Opening you up,
Fixing something,
And putting you back down gently.

It all leaves you better somehow,
Blossom-chested,
Swim-headed,
Dance-footed,
Different.

The Way the Dizziness Comes In

It starts with nothing, and in the end you have the wreckage of an orchestra, a houseplant, and 13 bathtubs full of honey twirling at the edge of your vision. And you have vocal cords that can make sounds even when they're silent. That's what it starts with:

Silence.

(You keep a handful of basketball courts on your shin). Then there's this quiet hum that rises all around you. (You keep a hornet behind your ear). It stands over you like a tree. (There are telephone wires running up your thighs). You want to hug it, but there is nothing to touch. (Your left eardrum has turned into a cactus). It feels like a desert shifting inside of you. (A mourning dove has made its nest in the nape of your neck). You think you are going deaf, but it is only because you have never heard music. (Blinking feels like a moth wanting).

Then it all starts to sound like matchbooks making love with flames. (You keep your scars inside your ribs). It is the sound of smoke. (Your knees have turned into garden hoses). Then all the pianos get angry. (Your throat is a bank vault). The sky decides to give up. (You learned to cry from your backbone). The ocean will not speak to you. (When you lay in your bed, you catch on fire).

The phone keeps telling you people are dying.
(Your heart is a book).
You are tired of phones.
(Your head is a carnival).

And just when you think you are going to fall down, you stand there, dripping water all over the bathroom tiles, looking at yourself in the mirror (butterflies are being born inside your wrist) and of all things, you smile.

That Aching Heartbeat That Stays With You Through It All

Some of us are eating hamburgers and some of us are forgetting to breathe. We get stumbling drunk, we talk to old friends in the street, children come from our wombs. We do what we can. We read sad stories in the newspaper, people sell us shoes, we register for library cards, elementary schools, elections. Sex drives us crazy, music creeps into our bodies and decides to stay. We do things we can't take back. We touch each other. We close our eyes and listen to the hum of the train. We stay in bed late some mornings. Our dreams haunt us. We cry sometimes, get mad at our parents, let ourselves fall in love. People we care about die. We try to be good.

All we are is a handful of freeze frames, set side by side, jumping like frogs, and nestling into each other, because nothing else makes sense.

Ducks Quack To Keep The Sadness Away

It is a fragile fabric we are woven from,
When you get to the real meat of the heart.
We all will become memories.
I wear my wrist
As a reminder.
The water will reach our necks
And keep going higher.
The wind will find us and begin to tear.
Fire cannot consume the same wood twice.
The ground will swallow us whole.
It is just one more reason
To paint colors across this day
As though our hands are brushes
And the spaces we move through
Just empty canvas
Begging for something beautiful
To be whispered into it.

These Rocks Can Read This Water the Way I Can Read A Book

Don't fall asleep, he says, the beggars are not the ones who are poor. The green of money is only an imitation of the plants it is printed upon, and it is hollow. Do not be fed by those hands, for they will leave you wanting.

Your heart is a canyon, he says. And his fingers are thin like lightning, and he points at the sky, and my eyes see enormous blue, mixed with silver visions of the thimbles we used to read about but never saw, and it feels like everything: orange trees, freeways, and winter, all of it, is rushing in toward me at the speed of books, and really all he is saying is that love, it's the biggest.

Listen, he says. And then he says nothing, and I hear nothing, and I say 'What?' and he says 'Shhh!' And then I hear the cicadas buzzing in the heat, and I hear my shin bones itching, and I hear the grass playing songs like the wind is an electric guitar, and I hear the way I used to hear when it was all a game we played on sunny days in boxes, like laughing was what we wanted to be when we grew up and dancing was a way of talking and my hand on your shoulder, in the frame-frozen grace of our innocence, meant Yes, Okay, Yes.

Feel your strength, he says. Feel it now for the times when you won't because sometimes the buildings might turn into trees throwing apples, and sometimes breathing might feel like drowning, and sometimes people will want to see you fail.

Let no one tell you 'You can't.' he says. When your heart beats it is saying 'It is time!' and when it stops it is saying 'Time is up!' and if it is time now, it may never be time again, which leaves you with nothing to say to someone else's doubt in you. The ribbons you trail behind you are cut from the mirrors our ghosts will look into to see if they did good, and the answer upon looking back can only be 'You were there. You did what was needed, and thinking on it too much now won't make it less true.'

Always dream, he says. There is not enough glue to hold onto all this Sadness and Love. Being alive is an earthquake trembling on the surface of a tear. We are only people, he says, and this is only a planet, sliding through emptiness and hoping a little bit that there might be more. There are quilts to be sewn, and there are people who have not been touched by gentle hands, and there are only four seasons but there is plenty to do in them. There is soil and growth, and don't forget about best friends.

I know you hurt, he says. Somebody dropped you before you were ready, and now your bruises have bloomed like strange flowers and you wear them like a shield, but
Snow is a miracle
And there is no such thing as can't,
And music,
Music is the greatest thing that we have ever done.

And then he says nothing.

And we stand there, and let the silence say what our words haven't yet learned how to, and then we turn and we walk home slow because our eyes have finished watching how miraculous the sun can make a moment, just by leaving it behind.

All Those Missing Pieces

Where he comes from, the light folds in on itself, looks like it's sleeping, like it's not even there, until it crashes into you, knocks you over, like you're just a person.

His father was a bricklayer. That's where he learned the trade. And by now his walls have grown too high for him to reach over and climb. Some days he spends with an ear glued to brick, listening for voices on the other side, and when he hears one, he tries to turn his fists into sledgehammers to smash through and prove he exists, but they aren't sledgehammers, they're just fists, and they bleed.

He knows the sound of the darkness whispering in his ear, like a cinder block in a blender. And he knows the feel of its hand on him, the one that turns him arctic every time. And he knows how to crumple beneath it like paper.

In the mirror he sees eyes shaped like icebergs, a smile sewn from steel. He knows his heart, it looks like a butcher shop. But he told the Can't Man to fuck off for good, I've had enough of your poison. He says, I'm not asking you to believe me, I'm only asking you to listen.

See, there are acres of orchards planted on his spine, and they ache like waitress feet, those tree bodies reaching up like arthritic hands trying to pray, and bloody knees bleeding sunset color.

The trees,
They grow,
From his back.

This man, he carries a forest with him. It's as if he's standing underwater the way he moves, surrounded by brick, and he thinks to himself:
If these walls could talk, they would scream.

He tells me he knows he's gonna have a daughter someday, so he's carving beneath his ribs now to slay the beasts that haunt him. They are not from him, or of him, but they are his to hold, glued together from the pain of the lives that created him, and he will not give his daughter to them.

He knows if the moon didn't shine on these rooftops, they would collapse upward. And if his feet didn't move, they would turn to grass beneath him.

He thinks of birds inside his shoulder blades. And that sledgehammer inside his fist. And he stands up against the flood. And he swallows an ocean. And he chews through a wall, brick by brick by brick, until he's just standing in the rain, on a streetcorner somewhere, soaked through but still breathing, and if he could stop laughing he would probably cry, because he knows that he has made it.

Cause where he comes from, the light, it folds in on itself, looks like it's not even there, until it shines on you, knocks you over, like you're nothing, but a person.

A Little Bit Human

The night is a strange museum,
And this tame wilderness,
These outcroppings of mountain bones
And half dead trees,
Are the best the city can do for ears
With which to listen to a man singing
On an empty street,
Bottle of whiskey half gone for the pain,
Voice like a handful of gravel
In the front pocket of a prayer.

Birds in Mid-Flight Over an Ocean of Enormous, Believing in the Place They Will Rest

Climb down into my ribs.
There is an aching.
Put on your boots for the dank and the wet.
Be sure to bring your tools.
Bring the adze, the auger.
Bring the hammer, the saw, and the level.
Bring wood.
There is much work to be done.
When you are inside, you will hear the rustling.
Light a match in the darkness.
You will see it, hulking there,
Quivering in the flickering chamber,
Wine-colored mass of pulp,
Whispering meat flailing in that humid cavern,
Murmuring in an alien tongue.
Build the scaffolding high.
Venture into the inner places.
You must ease your hands into the machinery,
Let it resonate through your bones.
Reach your hands in,
Gentle carpenter,
Tender surgeon,
And ply your trade.

Long Talks With Dead Friends

This is winter

Walking inside the trumpeting lonesome echoes
Of moonlight's lost lover
Ringing out along copper highways
In a midnight trill
The way dogs see with their noses

We bear unbearable losses
While our bodies become flooded cities
And our ears ring like felled trees

The world keeps on coming
And all our armor does nothing to protect us

Painting Pictures With Fire On Flammable Objects

The piano keys,
They are running through my blood,
Building monuments out of sound,
Translating the unbelievable fact of hammer
Put to work direct from physics to emotion.

I am small.
The waves toss my body like it is just a body
And the ocean is just the ocean.
I rumble along on the air currents
While secrets are whispered into my trapdoors.

I have heard the knock that blossoms
The blue doves into the open air
Like a door bursting open from a burning building,
Lungs heaving with empty thoughted animal knowing;
I know the pearls that cage themselves in campfires,
Only to be set free for that dying ecstasy of a glance.

The waiting is what kills us,
The spiteful thought
That there is something behind the veil that we cannot see.
It is the not knowing that we shed our tears for.
And the loss.

Occasional Tears

Bare and splayed-out open
In the dust drunk earth,
The brown expanse empty,
Just the naked dirt,
Begging for a single seed to be sown in it,
As it ever sits under the sky,
Waiting to do what it does,
Like a human heart
Laid bare,
Knowing even as the pain comes,
That it will not be the last time.

Mismatched Dust

A wild thing you are
How you blink smoke
And stare fire
With hands forged from dirt
And smile hewn from oak
Dragging yourself to the feet
Of your ferocious heart
In a land that no man calls home

Shout Stoutly at the Volume of Slow Motion Into My Somber Seashell Ears

In the fleeting forest of your glance,
My skin gives birth to a thousand buzzing bees.
I have seen men dig into the earth
And take residence of the sky.
I have seen the hacking and the hunger;
the quiet crowing of cities at twilight.
The life will be spilled from us yet.
We know this.
It is writ.
In all we do, there is a question.
A sailing ship.
A handful of bone.
Drunken wizardry.
The answers are why we continue.
And yea,
I am lost at sea most moments,
But when I am laying in the tall grass
Of the declining light,
With the bats beating blindly through the ether,
And the crickets breaking their own hearts
With the melancholy music of their bodies,
In those last few hours at least,
There is some comfort.

The Wishing Jar

Send them out.
Send them like soldiers to death.
Send them like children to dreams.
Send them like letters to love,
Like love to the person you need more than oxygen.
Send them like a better haircut to your sixth grade self
And a message that it will all get better someday.
Send them like parents to orphans,
Like a cure for AIDS,
Like a last conversation with someone you cannot get back.
Send them out like a gun that takes back bullets.

Fill the wishing jar.

Fill it and put it on the countertop in the kitchen
With the sunlight and the darkness
Just big enough to hold your childhood and just small enough
To fit Nebraska.

Fill it until it is full,
With cash, plane tickets and diamonds,
White picket fences and PTA meetings,
Strong sun and beaches,
The deed to a sunset, a secret door, soft skin, sex,
The seventh floor apartment,
A perfect body, violence or its end, death and its beginning,
Your own sky, a pregnant belly, the wings to fly,
And the music to march you home.

Fill the wishing jar with all you've got and then some
And then grab two fists full of soil,

Throw them on top
And then wait.
I cannot tell you what it will look like when it grows.
I can tell you mine was a tree
With limbs that had hands that would hold yours
And the fruit it bore held seeds shaped like hearts
Meant to be worn on sleeves.

I can tell you that what grows here
May be more than you can handle
And not what you want by the time you get it,
Though you once hoped for it
With heavy lids,
Cradled possibility like a stolen child.

My grandmother used to say to me
Shimmy,
Why don't you wish in one hand
And shit in the other
And see which fills up faster?
She was a nice lady.
But I don't recommend trying it.

Do not let someone else's words
Work your truth into an illusion.
The greatest visionaries
Are the ones who see what is not there,
But could be,
And build it.
The greatest visionaries are the ones who do
What everyone says cannot be done.

You are a dreamer.

I know because I am a dreamer and I have seen you,
Tied to a kite shaped like a cliff,
While a mockingbird sewed your wings back on,
And a fairy tale argued with you to be reasonable.
All our dreams are not rational.
They don't have to be.
All you can do is know what you know,
And love what you love,
No matter what so-called authority tries to tell you otherwise.
And learn that things may be as they must be.

You can take more than you think you can.
Like a broken leg,
Or getting fired,
Or falling in love again

The wishing jar is not there to make your wishes come true
It is only there to hold them
Until you decide to.

Teaching Angels How to Breathe Like Touching

Burn bright.
She told me to burn bright.
We all have to burn a little, she said,
It's just a part of all this,
But when it's your turn,
Let the pain of the flames that consume you
Also be the fuel that moves you.
Flames have a tendency to engulf,
But burning in light is better than drowning in darkness,
So move your body like you are gasoline
And everyone you encounter is a lit match,
Let your prayers be crackling embers
Exhaled up to kiss the stars.
All this living is bound to hurt some, she said,
So we might as well make the hurt worth something.

In Search of Everywhere

Sock puppet moon
With newsprint eyebrows
All perfumed with surprise
As the ceiling floods away.
Night like a violin.
Flickering room,
Hovering around makeshift skin,
Throat like a windchime singing heaven
Eyes like mouths
Devouring books
In this prison of light.

2

What If Our Guts Don't Know Anything and We've Been Listening To Them All Along?

Streetlights Don't Blink When You Say I Love You

My grandmother was strong and crazy.
She's dead now.
Cancer.
I still feel the rasp in her voice,
The stale cigarette smell of her car,
The blue veins pressing out against the skin on the back of
Her hands,
The way we spun and spun
And how it seemed like we would never
Stop
When she ran that red light.
My sister was crying in the back seat.
My grandmother complained of pain in her neck.

I couldn't have been more than 9 or 10
But in the silent shock of the aftermath,
There was the incredible certainty
Of knowing death was standing behind my left shoulder,
That he reached out
And ruffled my hair,
Then just turned and walked away.

My Dead Grandfather Standing in the Dining Room

After the cancer took his leg, and
the chemo took his hair, and
after he turned into a bouquet of bones
wrapped up in crepe paper skin,
Death finally got around to killing him,
and then one day,
as I was walking out of the kitchen,
there he was,
waving and smiling,
like it was the most natural thing in the world.

My Father, On the Eve of His Birth, 57 Years to The Day

Whiskey drunk, we stumble onto the dock
And watch the sea crawl toward us on its belly,
Whispering and screaming at the same time.
He speaks as though he is a forest burning down.
I am mostly silent.
He says, "a birthday is just another day."
I think to myself, "I am glad you were born."

The String Plucking Nostalgia

feet planted like daisies
in the bottom of a pair of boots,
slinging toe tapping rhythms on the road
with a thumb at the sky.
ill be your blazing blue streak,
death on two legs,
sweet-talking,
tune-whistling,
traverser of these american roads.
god bless it!
i got something in me, and it grows.
sometimes it blooms and sometimes it sits.
it makes me strong and crazy.
it presses its fingers against my heart
and i feel it furiously,
bruising ferocious
in one of those tin can afternoons
with that toothpaste sunset blinking at me,
calling out apocalypse litanies
on the hoarse throat of the wind,
careening in every direction at once,
building inside me like a house
until my lungs turn into boxing gloves,
and just when i think i might explode,
it always goes calm again.
it always goes calm.

The Never-Was Sailor

Standing on the deck, staring out over a calm sea, like eternal pancakes running forever to four horizons; hoisting the sails to bleed white in the sunset and carry wind in their frenetic palms; aching through the long lonely isolation of that enormous blue wilderness, while my beard pokes further from my face and my heart hurts with the dull shock of longing; thirst floating dangerous on an ocean of undrinkable water; a triumphant return from far lands to my wife and children, and the rise up of that blood feeling like electric eels inside of me, ecstatic, before the old itch returns and I feel the pull of the sea once more: these are all the things I have never felt, because my legs have not left land for long enough. I am a sailor who never was.

Business as usual

As I walked out of the gym at one in the morning on a Friday night, after running in place on a machine for a few miles, which is something I do sometimes, I saw a carton of milk launch from the window of a speeding sport utility vehicle, miss the stumbling drunken teenagers it was aimed at, and explode on the sidewalk behind them. They looked confused and ridiculous and not as afraid as they should have been. Then, down the block, a man was standing in the middle of the street with an overturned bicycle, which he repeatedly picked up and smashed on the ground, over and over and over again, screaming "This tire is a piece of shit! This! Tire! Is a piece of shit!" It was unclear whether he was screaming it to me or to himself, but I just kept walking, deciding it was best not to find out. When I got home the palm trees were silhouetted against the clouds. My first thought: "Who does that?" My second thought: "Man, life is weird."

A History Lesson

There was a brief period of a few generations, several hundred years ago, (in remote regions of what are now Russia and the Czech Republic), during which it was believed by doctors and scientists that blood flow to the head was of utmost importance, and thus people began teaching their children to walk on their hands from a young age. Slowly, over time, the culture was completely transformed. Eventually most of daily life was carried out upside down, and the entire society was run from the hands up. Everything was made to conform to the demands of hand walking. Special glove-like shoes were created for the hands. Fashion trends developed. Social customs were radically changed. Agility and dexterity walking on the hands became a prized quality in a mate. The norm subtly altered itself. In time, it was considered rude to be seen in public walking on one's feet. People would scoff and hurry away (on their hands, of course). Only on formal occasions, such as weddings or funerals, did people concede to walk upright, and only then in the name of ritual and tradition. However, even on such occasions, small children would invariably still be seen running around and playing on their hands. But people generally accepted this with good humor because after all, the children were still young, and had not yet learned the ways of the world.

It Is Hard to Let Yourself Be Loved

This is the way it must feel for a flower,
Pushing itself out from the green,
With a violence of color,
In a swirling moment of pain and passion.

Flowerpot

The nights are football field long,
and I find myself in the middle of them,
walking.

A Memory

Eating peach pie on the patio of a run-down highway cafe, and watching the rain fall on a roadside farm with my old true love, while she drank decaffeinated tea and told me about Russia and her fiancé, and we tried to pretend our hearts weren't reaching for each other from out our chests.

I remember feeling vaguely sick to my stomach, and thinking I had eaten too much pie. I told her I had never seen a cornfield, and she, being her, took me to her favorite one, and ran off in the corn. When I caught her, out of breath and laughing, it was the first time we had touched in years, and the corn was an electric swaying all around us, and I should have kissed her but didn't.

Instead the moment ended, and we walked back to the car, like it was the most mundane thing in the world, like we were doing our taxes, dragging the past behind us like a heavy kitchen appliance, not realizing how big the sky was above us.

Temporary Insanity

Tonight I saw two people
Walking down the street
Wearing motorcycle helmets.
There was not a motorcycle in sight.
The fact that there were two of them,
Coupled with the fact
That there was no one else around,
Made it seem entirely normal.
And the fact that it seemed normal
That they were wearing helmets
Made them seem like space aliens.
And the fact that deep down I knew
That they were not space aliens,
But rather human beings,
Made them seem like friendly space aliens.
And this gave me hope.

My Grandmother's Coffin

It was lighter than I expected,
like moving a dining room table,
except more sad.

3

The Dream Architects Are Coming

I Believe In The Existence of Strawberries

There are turtles sleeping in a garden somewhere
While candles burn on top of their shells
And an old record plays the blues
And two people dance
As though one of their bodies is the sky
And the other
The storm sweeping across it.

The Mind is the Heart's Attic

Life is wearing a red polka dot dress and high heels made of skyscrapers. She's blowing on a trombone like a dragon speaking words made of barbecue at the village's bravest knight. The trombone is red hot, shaped like a ballerina and smoking a cigarette. She has feet like the fastest Vincent Blackshadows you ever saw and eyes like migrating butterflies.

Death has a crush on life.

Death is holding a golf putter over his shoulder and taking a sip of warm orange juice. He's staring straight at life with narrowed eyes and tapping foot. Death wants to dance, but doesn't. He has hands like oak trees on fire. His chest is watery like a seahorse dreaming about being a pelican. Death wants life like tattoos want skin.

The music she plays is a river full of swimming. Everyone is doing the jitterbug, going mad, in a haze of twilight and dust, with twirling lighthouse heads and kitchen appliance legs going completely insane like a kiss on the lips. Each face is a smile factory. Life is grinning like god damn.

And ashes to ashes,
We all
Fall down.

Stomachs Are Not Vacation Places For Food

Sometimes when the birds sound particularly lovely outside in the trees, singing against the overcast sky, I flip myself over so that I can walk around on my hands, and, if it's even possible, they sound somehow lovelier. What is happening inside my brain is this:

At first all the red inside me moves like slow motion snails, and for an instant that seems like a moment that is really just a second, all the squishy gadgets inside me are wondering just what the hell is going on, and then my veins turn into roller coaster rides for my blood, and every single blood cell has its hands in the air, going round the loops and turns and screaming 'Whoooooaaaaaaaa!" And then wham! All at once they cram into my brain like spelunkers dropping into some sort of upside down, underground cave and their sudden entrance creates a momentary vacuum which results in a sonic boom that instantly eradicates all the thoughts that are normally careening around in my head like futuristic Tokyo hovercraft traffic, and in that miniscule fraction of a second that is already pulling away from me train-like, my ears open up a little wider and convey that far off singing to my brain a little clearer, and those little tiny creatures singing their great big songs, that used to just be the backdrop to my all-important existence, have suddenly become the purpose of the whole entire thing.

I Think Bees Have Got The Right Idea

Just imagine
That your job
Is to rub your entire body
On a flower one hundred times your size
All so you can go home at the end of the day
And make honey.

Clearing My Throat Like a Chainsaw So's I Can Whisper Quiet Enough

I have made a pile of mailboxes in the front yard.
My theory is that sending someone a mailbox
Is much more meaningful
Than sending them a letter.

It is more of a production.

Of course
You can always put a letter in the mailbox
Before you send it.

It Pours Like Polyester Rain in a Desert of Style

You stitch the seams unruly,
Glide the cloth onto your frame with care
And move calm through a swirl of moving bodies
With a wink and a blown kiss
In a slow spin that resembles gambling.
Your movements are slow motion flowers,
And the cloth explodes around your skin
In bursts of color,
Like you are wearing the fourth of July on your back.
This is no fairy tale.
You are true.
I have seen you.
And you are true.

God's Fingers On the Spine of Autumn

There is a certain perverse beauty
Within the slow strangling desiccation
That ever accompanies the whistling rhythms
Arranging and rearranging themselves so resolutely
Inside midnight's blinking posture.

Just beyond the frigid air forcing itself upon the starlight,
There is warmth.
It is beneath my brown corduroy blankets.
I will meet you there.

Penis Sunburn

Ouch!

The Most Lovely Left Shoelace In The City

It is glorious, my god!
It is as though the sky dripped saliva in a long string,
The sun high-fived it with three rays of sunlight,
Venus gave it a wink and it ended up in your left shoe.
My sweet lord, it is magnificent!

Two Parts of the Same Thing
For Lauren Shomaker

Part One

If you were to take 500 gallons of red paint
And put it on a papier maché heart the size of Canada
Surround it with all the laughter you've ever heard
Mixed with the way you feel
When you see an adorable puppy dog
And the look on your face
The first time you saw the ocean
Multiplied by the freedom birds must feel
When they step off a branch into air
And instead of falling
They fly
Or perhaps a gazelle
Running through some really tall grass
Screaming "Hell yeah Mother Hubbard, I'm hella fast!"
That kind of freedom
Or the freedom you feel
When your soul expresses itself bodily
In the form of the way you danced that one time
To that one song
When you let go completely
Like a mind, body, and soul
Or-Ga-Sm!
Now if you take all that
Cover it in gasoline
Light it on fire
And transform it all into an emotion
You have about 3 percent of what I feel my heart do
When I see you smile.

Part Two

Falling in love is like willingly throwing yourself on a grenade. Except the grenade looks like an adorable puppy dog. So you dive on the ground and roll around with it. You tell yourself, "It probably won't explode, because how could something so innocent-seeming be dangerous?" And then BAM! It explodes and shatters your ribcage and damages all of your vital organs. And if you really fell hard, then when you're standing there, holding your intestines, with shrapnel in your chest, and the doctor's telling you how long you have, you're nodding and saying "Yeah, I know Doc. But it was worth it!" Yeah, love is Awesome. I mean, otherwise why would we put ourselves out there? It's not as if we don't know all the risks. Half of all the movies, books, and songs, ever made were motivated by heartbreak. Just go rent that crappy 80s movie "Say Anything," with John Cusack where he stands outside her window with a boombox, playing "Your Eyes" and totally gets shot down! And if John Cusack can get shot down, is there really hope for the rest of us!? I used to wonder about that a lot, but the answer is "Fuck John Cusack, there is hope!" Because even if someone went demolition derby on your heart. Even if they ripped it out with a rusty clothes hanger and put it on a stake in the town square for all the villagers to see, it's true, it was probably worth it. And you would do it all again. Because you have to take that risk. You have to see. Because if you would take it back, it wasn't love.

nighttime water faucet

my throat
is like a riverbed
that hasn't had
a river in it
for a
long time
but wants to.

haiku, sort of

giant robot
quietly eats my face
in the early morningtime

Trenches Our Hearts Have Dug

Before this,
I was just hands kissing pockets in the night,
Before.
Just a restless junkyard piano dog,
Fuming like a declaration of war.
I was just
Dead life,
Killing time,
Before.

And then it was the horrible shame
Of losing eating contests,
Punk Rock and Frank Sinatra,
And the moon,
Being itself again.

It was flames across the room
The size of the Brooklyn Bridge,
A bit like drowning.
It was the prettiest war yet.
A plane, an open hatch,
A falling bomb,
And a cloud shaped like a mushroom.

It was
First kiss
Apocalypse.

Time was you'd find me in a moonlit bedroom,
Swirling drunk with your scent,
Keeping warm at your body,

Furnace that you are,
And every inch of skin, a bullhorn,
Screaming for touch.

So be my strings
And dance me.
Dance me steady like waves.
Dance me hard like street.
Dance me slow like honey-suckle.
Dance me crazy like straitjacket.

Move me in clock steps
With star-pasted eyes.
Because if seeing is believing
Then touching is the altar
Where believers worship

And when I touch you, I feel religious.

Some days inscribe themselves to your parts.
It's as if they autograph your bones,
And there's that workshop clamor inside your chest,
Those buzz saws beneath your skin start to spinning.

Behind my eyes it will always be:
Scarf Grab Chapstick Kiss.
On the bottom of my mouth:
Tongue Swirl Cinnamon Taste.
On the inside of my wrist:
Run Scream Laughing
With Belly Ache From Funny
All Umbrellaless
And Wet With Sky Water.

But I've run out of legs to carry me now,
So I will sail on, until I sink
And when those shadows fall
I'll grow me a sailor's beard,
Leave these rotten cliffs
For the companionship of the sea.
Bring your fanciful tridents and let me sink!
I'll find my death with watery eyes,
Blink back the whole of the ocean's salt tears,
Sucker punch the moon
With a brass knuckle gaze,
Dream of you dancing on Churchbell Sundays,
All mud and silk,
Swimming through cornfields
Like a last kiss
That desperately wants to happen,
But never will.

Because you and I,
We are running from always
And we will spend the rest of our lives
Trying to catch our breath from the rooftops,
Hearing unexpected music,
Noticing the flowers that remind us of each other,
With that feeling in the guts
Like running full speed downhill,
And the sky tilting slightly to the left,
All the while wondering
If we were ever truly
Awake.

On the Nights When the Moon is Like the Sky's Brain Thinking Too Much

This poem is temporarily closed for repairs.
We apologize for any inconvenience
This may have caused.

When the Future Looked Like a Cartoon, the Bellowing Was Faint, But Now That the Future is a Fist Inside an Anthill, the Bellowing is an Empty Belly

When the dust settled, our guns were rusted over. The man at the bar had a pile of dirt and daisies in place of his eighteen year grin. The arriving twelve o'clock train sounded like a pregnant woman in hard labor. We didn't move at all. For three hundred years we stood there. The time felt like sand on the back of my neck, grains shifting, moving, blowing in the wind. The saloon collapsed around us. They built an enormous city where the town used to be. Folks seemed to be under the impression that we were great works of art. At some point I moved again. The people around me seemed pretty shook up. My mouth tasted like cactus death. I sure could have used a beer. Out of nowhere a massive snarling mechanical beast came roaring by. It surprised me. Caught me off guard is all. 'What in sam-hill is that?' I said. 'It's a car,' said one of the silly-ass looking people who had begun to gather around and stare. Well, I didn't know what a 'car' was. 'Aren't you a statue?' said another one. 'Son,' I said, 'I've tore off a man's hand and fed it to him for less than what you just said to me.' He didn't say much after that.

The Eternal Ham Sandwich

The truth was hard to bear,
So we just ignored it,
Played the games,
Went along as though it was
The most natural thing in the world.
But in the end,
We all turned into cabbages,
Rolling around on the concrete
Of a vacant parking lot.

4

The Last Days Of The Goldfish Kid

As the Hive Grows to the Brink of a Straitjacket

We are elephants at heart.
But we are as smart as pianos.
All this pushing and no calm.
There is a festering madness growing inside of us.
We do all the wrong things,
But we don't know any better.
So we scramble for the only lights that can save us.
Love or Kindness or Imagination.

Blame Needs A Triceratops To Hold it

Swing below the clouds with a refrigerator for a fist
And blank canvas the migraine of the modern conscience
With the weight of listening.
You are what the world needs.
It is a simple song if only you could hear it.
You could learn to sing it
If only you had the patience.

A Quilt Shaped Like Your Hands

Telephone poles are a city's misguided way
Of trying to touch the sky.
The traffic is thick,
It moves like an artery.
The cars paw the road,
They don't think about how
The ceiling inside the vein is painted like apples,
Making a sound similar to gravel.
What I am trying to do is make sense
At the edge of heaven,
Like the burning dreams of trees
That hold light inside their wood.
Their laughter rings like gravity
And it will never stop.
Not even after they become telephone poles,
Especially not then.

The Last Day of the American Century

Don't look at me,
I'm ugly.

The Children That The Ache Brings

She sits on the porch,
Her rocking chair creaking
Where the wood joins itself together
Like a handshake between trees.
The wind blossoms from the west
And brings us the scent of ash,
Carrying it into our throats so that every swallow
Has the taste of dead fire.

My feet are bare on the painted planks of the porch,
Fitting to grow roots and plant me in this doorway.

She is wearing that blue dress
That has always reminded me of drowning
And she is beautiful.
She looks up at me,
With her belly full of birth,
And I watch her grow ferocious,
Her eyes pushing on me, fist-like.

Neither of us speaks.
She has not spoken to me in months.
And I do not have the words.
How is it that my body has mixed with hers
And fitted this child into her womb?

Her chair creaks and my head mumbles
As the old prayer runs through me.
When and wherefore will the sky assign us our wings?

She says nothing.

And as our eyes set together in the silence,
My mind moves,
Her chair creaks and I am lost in the sound,
And I think of all of us
Stuck here on this earth
Like as with the swamp mud about our legs.
We remain still while the land moves around us
And we are beholden to the ache,
As the seconds sprawl out beyond us
Until the daily is through,
And our faces grow drawn and long and grey.

The turning goes on and we know it
But don't let it seep in.
We plastic ourselves from the world
And toil in it side by side,
Thrashing about mute,
With our legs in the mud,
Taking in the measure of each other's pain
Through the eyes
With no words and no mind but loss,
And no able to break it,
Just the long lessons hollowed into death,
Echoing in our ears
As we break our teeth on the hard-bitten truth.

These wicked machines
They have got their hands into us,
Stirring up cancers and melancholy
As we grow lost to ourselves,
Stuck and burning, hands full of fire.
And carrying the flames into the night we lie ourselves down
Beneath the moon,

Our bodies heaving in the whispering dark
And we close our eyes,
While in the harbor
And in the cornfields,
And in the empty bellies,
All our ships are slowly sinking.

And yet,
In spite of it all,
There is the unlikely boon of each day rising,
Lined up colorful next to all the other days
And brought to bear in uniform splendor.
It pleases a man right well
To feel the sweat on his back over the course of a day
And see his work packed in piles to the south of the known sky.
It pleases a man right well
To bleed into the soil and know
That it is not without consequence,
As the blood in our veins
Does not begrudge us our time here.
To know the shape of his tears and his muscles
And the forms they wrap themselves around
Knowing that it is the moments
We do not think to remember that we do.
It pleases a man right well.

The creaking of her chair comes from a long way off,
Breaks my reverie,
And brings me back to the porch,
Her eyes still on me.

I move dream-like, and sit beside her,
Departing the empty white,

Like as the color green come into being
For the first time,
Still unknown to itself,
With the child of our accidental making
Growing even now in her womb.

We tumble together down a long tunnel of silent seconds
And come out the other end holding hands.
Her eyes are softer now.
Our touching is like a century.

The love I have to bear her comes from a long way
Across a desert of human history,
The broken backs of horses,
And the feet of starving children,
With the knowledge that we have all stained each other
Irrevocably.

Her rocking chair creaks
And her tears come the same time as her smile
As for the first time in months
She opens her mouth to speak.

Self-Fulfilling Prophecy

Oh those salted wounds of the doomed battles we wrongly hurled ourselves into that no history will remember right and no one will sing songs of, with their taste of iron and smoke, marking our guilty flesh with false memories of the bodies of friends loved ones and strangers, left and lost lingering in our dark places, wearing death masks and painting with finger paints over the gaping eight year holes the images of their never to be lived futures, their could have beens, and the child faces their ever closed eyes will not see again.

We Are All Going To Die From Something

Do you ever wonder what kind of undies the president wears?
Me neither.
I was just asking.

Tying Knots (The American Way)

Lonely,
We dig holes in the earth.
Yearning,
We point telescopes at the stars.
Pleading,
We drink ourselves into sleep.
Longing,
We work ourselves into caskets.
We believe in futures
That probably will not be.
We idealize pasts that weren't quite
The way we remember them.
But we will be free.
We will get ours
If we have to kill everyone to do it.

The Death Of The News

When books go extinct,
I will replace my eyes with computers
And my ears with speakers.
I will have my heart surgically removed
And I will replace it with nothing.
I will think about how much progress we have made.

The Axe is Making Out With The Tree While We Look The Other Way

We have grown extension cords from our spines,
Replaced our teeth with computer chips,
Learned the rhythm of a synthetic heartbeat
And now we dance to it.
Our pulse swings predictably wild,
A regulated bloodstream of binary code.
It all adds up very efficiently.
The numbers are exact.
You can calculate them to the last decimal.

But there are still green things growing from the ground.
Blossoms still explode scent and color in ecstasy every spring.
The sea is still salty.
The sun still shines burning.
The desert will still pound you breathless with its silence.
Animals still sniff the brown earth,
Inhaling the damp richness
Of roots and leaves and decay and growth.
We still eat,
Still breathe,
Still make love like wilderness,
Taste the sweat,
Collapse in mutual exhaustion,
Lungs heaving like pianos,
Reaching to hold the air
In quivering arms.

Artificial Wind Blowing on Artificial Lovers Making Artificial Love Beneath an Artificial Tree

We are warped creatures, the lot of us. We drag our claws along the concrete and breathe our moans like sea lions. We stitch up our chests with fishing line and burn good mahogany to cook scraps of rot. It is a junkyard pile of dust that we have built for ourselves, in spite of our craving to lie upon unsoiled mattresses, away from cities of trash, to scrape our flesh clean and wear new costumes for a day. We are not all that terrible, we human beasts. We are just lonely and don't know how to show it.

We just want to dream a little, without being scolded for it.

If I Kiss You Where it's Sore

There is a man in the boiler room,
Who keeps it all moving,
Red faced and sweating.
His fingers are the size of staplers.
His biceps are like the bulging roots of an oak tree.
He pushes and pulls the levers and pulleys,
Blisters his hands,
And billows the fires to grow mountains,
To engineer car crashes,
To burst small clouds into ten thousand raindrops,
To bring my thumbs up to brush away your tears.
When they kitchen sink your back,
Replant the volume inside unfamiliar music,
And set a pack of dogs to sleep around you like flames,
Take solace,
You are a stronghold,
And with the push of a lever,
You can become a dove again.

5

To Give Myself To You In a Handful Of Honest

Giraffe Tongues Leave a lot of Room For Being Speechless

For Melody Rose Thompson Stone

Butterflies sleep inside her collarbones.
I have seen them dreaming.
It looks like a sunset painting itself across her shoulders.
She walks like leaves rustling.
Her body is a flowerbed.

When I touch her skin,
I know that I must have been a tree once.
It is the only way I could have learned
The patience it takes
To go about a day,
Doing anything
Other than
Touch her.

Let's Be Mountain Goats Together

I wish to sleep beneath your sky tonight,
Inside a room filled with lamps
Confusing to the senses,
Shining a light that looks like summer heat
As our mouths make fast friends of each other
Within walls sewn together from the stems
Of blooming flowers.
There is no blood in me.
When we speak
I fill up with your words
And they course through my veins.
They find my arteries.
They swim through me like goldfish.
They like it there.

Kissing Your Neck is Something I Would Like to Make a Career Out Of

It will be a simple life but a good life. I will wake up mornings. Sip a cup of black coffee. Eat a nice breakfast, maybe a bagel. Put on a tie and coat and take the train to work. On the way I will do a crossword puzzle. Or a sudoku. When I get to work, I will hang up my coat, roll up my sleeves, sit down at my desk, and begin a long day of kissing your neck.

I will kiss your neck 8 hours a day, 5 days a week, for 37 years. It will pay moderately, but the job has its own perks. It is pay enough in itself. I will be so good at kissing your neck that my managers will notice. They will want to promote me. They will want to pay me more. I will advance quickly through the company. They will want me to kiss your neck all the time. They will say no one has ever kissed your neck quite as well as I do. They will congratulate me, slap me on the back, and shake my hand. They will buy me a scotch after work.

And it will go on this way for years and years, until I am old and begin eating my dinner at 4 o'clock in the afternoon. And then one day, I will retire. I will be sad to go, but it will be time. I will feel like I have really given something back, like I have really made my contribution. The company will give me a good pension, enough to live on, and with all the extra time I have, I will feed ducks in the park, and make conversation with strangers in coffee shops, and reflect on my life. I will wander the streets, lost and confused, void of purpose. I will spend some late nights, up alone at the kitchen table, staring out the window and wondering how the time has passed so quickly. I will think about you.

Ultimately, I will be unable to stay away. And in my spare time, and quiet moments, though it has been years of it, day in and day out, I will probably still end up spending most of my time kissing your neck.

The Book Trials

Book 1.
The beehive is buzzing beneath my skin.
I am zippering up the last melodies
To fold up and bed beneath for the winter.
Be a tree for me,
Sling your sap sticky over my tongue.
Stain the shadows in sweet phosphorescence,
And caress the wind with your whispering needles.

Book 2.
When I was a child,
My father used to cut my hair.
Our kitchen turned into a barber shop those afternoons.
I remember thinking what a talented dad he was,
That he knew how to cut hair,
But did something else for a living.

Book 3.
My girl has a body like a fire truck:
Like a childhood dream.
When I kiss her, I become the numbers above the elevator,
Switching every floor.
Our lips touch and the doors open,
And every number I am, I glow.

The Myth Of Light

Your kisses fling disembodied birdsongs through me
Like I am a basement staircase
That cinderblocks are crashing down,
Into a darkness that is heavy
With rusted bicycles,
Old birdcages,
And teenage memory.
It is an engulfing darkness,
Shaped like the insides of your arms.

If human-kind is a flurry of short-lived self-importance,
Creating monuments to its own destruction,
Reaching to extinguish the light,
Then I will walk like a clam,
Straight into the darkness,
Holding your hand in mine like a rare treasure.

Eyes like Skyscrapers on Fire

For centuries we have slept in strange beds,
Gone digging for the stars in empty pockets
While unseen overhead
They came on like porch lights.
We have heard that voice from beyond the throat
Tearing out like a cello
At the frequency of cracking icebergs,
Shuddering for a response.

We have felt the edge of winter like a blade,
Held our bodies to the lions,
And through the darkness
That leaks from beneath the bones
To build the risen towers
Of our least credible dreams,
We have rampaged
And stalked shivering back,
With shells in our hair,
Sea-swallowed and hungry,
Blistered and broken,
Unceasing and unrelenting,
Toward the only thing that mattered:

Where your skin first touched mine,
Fire was born.
The city where we met still burns,
Look to the smoke and see.
For we are consumed with the flames
As in a lover's eyes
And look you all the buildings do burn.
All the past has been just prologue to this:

On the night of the day that I first kissed you
I wore my lips like pearl handled pistols,
Walked with Mercutio's swagger,
Held my head up as though it were the sky itself,
And proclaimed thus to the pigeons:

'Buckle my knees and spin the world.
Give me the breath, the words, a thought.
Give me a mountain, a flame, a kiss.
A moment or eternity.
Turn the sky black in mid-afternoon.
Empty out my heart like an old purse
So I may fill it with you.
For I will know no more days like this one.'

One day our bodies will lie beneath this ground.

But dear heart, hear me.
As the redness drips every second closer to black
With the deep pounding,
Discovering you in the chaos,
Like a blaze in a blizzard,
Has warmed me.

When my eyes lose the power to see,
I will be glad they had the chance to fall into yours
And should I grow lost,
I will find my way
Through the kisses like light
That you toss for me to catch
As a hopeful bride does flowers.

We are made from pieces of all things

And one day our parts,
As scattered dust,
Will mingle above some far ocean.
And on that day,
Though we no longer have lips,
You will once again
Know my kiss.

Sex, Like Death, Like Apples

It always starts with a word.
A syllable or two,
Just a guttural hurricane stumble,
The larynx boiling over,
That primal vibration earthquaking the throat,
With the molecules rubbing each other tectonic
Between two lips and an ear:
"Hi.
It's nice to meet you."
And then in another moment,
Another now,
I am tasting the sweat of your inner thigh.

In exploring the topography of your body
I have become a mapmaker.
The canyons of your finger prints,
The hint of blue beneath your wrist,
The hollows of your hips,
They are the moment that the beat drops,
They are a painting that can stop me in my tracks,
They are the ways we have taught each other
To build light.

We are rhythm, movement, and measure.
Call me clock, and you time,
And let my hands move inside of you.

They are selling fruit in the marketplace.
Pears that drip.
Mangoes sweet to the tongue.
Your tongue is in my mouth.

Someone is rowing on the harbor,
Muscles taut,
The sweat between his shoulder blades.
You taste like the sea.
The white curtains billow from the open window.

Somewhere a tomato, pierced by a knife,
Gushes its juices
Onto a wooden cutting board.
Our clothes are grinning at us from the floor.
A garden is growing in slow motion.
Your breasts are rushing toward my tongue.
The scent of lavender is lifting through the open window.
Your skin is growing goosebumps.
The ocean is swaying its hips.
A seahorse thinks
A beehive behaves
Your nakedness surprises me.
In the next room
A telephone is ringing.

I want you.

At a middle school dance
Two kids sway together
Without ever hearing the music
That is playing all around them.
Their stomachs touch like electrocution.
The air is swollen with heat.
A mockingbird shreds the night
With a song drenched so heavy in sweetness
That the heart swoons to hear it.
The room is melting around us.

Your back is arching
In the slanted light of afternoon
Through the window of an empty kitchen
Two dust motes chase each other
Around and around
But they will never touch.

Your orgasm is the fall of Troy.

You gasp
Your body jerks and spasms
With the dying throes of Achilles
There are gunshots in the distance
We both hold our breath as flames lick the walls

A moan escapes you
Echoing the screams
Of the murdered innocent
From the street
The wail of an infant

Across town a paramedic
Presses his palms
To a man's chest wound
Trying to hold the life inside
From spilling out
It is all in the touch
All our muscles are tensed

Priam is weeping
To watch his great city burn
The sweat glistens on our skin
We are welded together

Through the wall
We can hear the laugh track
Of the neighbor's television
Our eyes are locked like a bank vault
I have not used this body until now

Paris returns his arrows to their quiver
And you shiver in the exposed air

And for just
A single
Moment
The silence is absolute

And then
We breathe again.

Hear Me When I Say This
For Kellee English

All the rooms, closets, and cupboards of your body
Are house and home to the self-same knowledge as this:

If I look
At the yellow combs around which buzz
The breathing bridal chambers
Of each bursting blossom
In the midst of its most tender act,
Blazing like guns
With sex and color
To produce the sweetest honey,

If I touch the moon's iris,
Curling full with its own luminosity
In a month long slow-motion blink,
Or wink,
All things move my feet in your direction.
You are true north.
And I follow the quivering needle of my compass without
question.

It is as if all the spaces I inhabit,
And all that inhabits me,
Is climbing a ladder of light
Toward the engines of your waiting orchestra.

If your eyes see to be madness
Those fluttering fragments of dust and dreams
Which I hold as my own,
And you decide

To leave me released
In those same fields in which you found me,
Remember,
That my roots may grow in many soils.

But if time's tangle sees fit to bind us,
With each other's taste ever on the other's tongue,
If twilight's crickets seek your ear
In which to whisper their sweetest melodies
And find my own,
You shall find none as apt and willing as I.

My love,
Beloved,
Will caress itself onto your skin.
And no matter where your traveling feet may take you,
In this world
Or any other,
You will find it already there,
Waiting for you.

The Fruit That Grows Into A Washing Machine Haircut

The blues man is holding his guitar like it is a marriage.
He is really belting it out,
And the ripples of music are on the verge of melting
All the buildings for blocks around.
He is inventing rock and roll
With his eyes closed
And fingers like an eggbeater,
Doing the eternal equation
That translates music into movement,
Where X equals the rhythm of the bassline
And Y equals the distance between two bodies.
You have summer in your hair
And you are wearing that yellow dress
That forces me to imagine you naked
And it seems only right and proper
That we have wild sex
Right here
In this laundromat.

To Wrap Arms About The Sunset's Daughter

Tell your dreams to me.
I want to know the way the colors enfold you.
I can see you sleep-eyed and slurring beneath
The white summer sheets,
Your smile a blessing in some unfamiliar language,
Your body a dream the flowers have forgotten.
I would like a bouquet of you to decorate my rooms.
I would like that just fine.

The Melody of a Rose

we will send a barrage of sleeping dump trucks
against the entrance to twilight,
barge in,
bleed it dry of color,
refuse to leave,
and then ask its forgiveness.

we will wear dining room tables on our backs,
spend all day in the kitchen,
cook a feast,
and feed ten thousand hobos,
we will ask an oak tree to touch its toes,
wash the tired feet of an ambulance driver,
perfume the neck of imagination,
become best friends with smiling,
make love in the streets,
push misery to the floor,
sit on its chest
and teach it tenderness.

we will wrist watch the time man
until his pace-maker becomes a heart.

the silence will close in
but we will be thick enough to hold it,
bearing candles into the library of night.
and we will watch the silhouette of the sky
against whatever is bigger than the sky
that our eyes are too fragile to decipher,
as it presses itself,
bursting affection,

nuzzling the tired shoulders
of that great beast
that sits just above our recollection,
too big to touch,
too far to reach,
but always there,

you,
you have a smile that breaks sunsets in half,
and causes my heart to origami itself every time.

you surprised me,
reminded me that i have a body,
awoke me from a great slumber,
and now i can't possibly sleep anymore
and it feels so good to come awake.

so kiss me,
while polar bears drown,
and politicians circus themselves,
and bullets carry names unwarranted to death.
while youth still beats in these bodies,
kiss my lips,
that love may decorate every word i speak from them.

spell for me the words that this world is forgetting
as daily we hear history's thunder
in the false skies that have been erected.
i will set my glasses to my eye
so that i may make out the many barrels
of the many guns that are being pointed.
the smoke is rising like ghosts
and none can say how much time is left.

in the unwinding black of dawn
the horses are screaming.
we hunch low,
lean forward,
backs straight,
knees grasping,
and the horizon advances so close
we can see the hilt of its knife.

the swan dive moment kisses the bottom,
caresses our collar bones,
and leaves us reeling,
hallucinating music,
thinking about the color blue
as though falling a great distance,
from a great height
where up is not a direction,
but an emotion
and the sky is nothing
but a color you can recognize
inside the moments before you fall to sleep.

you,
you are snow,
a claw-foot bathtub,
bullet shells.

the storm above glows a soft violet
we are breaking off our footsteps behind us.
as i reach for your hand,
i ask where we are going,
and you smile and say to me
that we have always walked in these woods

we just haven't remembered yet
and as the clouds part you point to the moon
and my body gets that gentle, slow feeling
like all my blood has just turned to honey inside my veins

and the rain,
when it finally falls,
it never makes a sound.

The Uneventful Apocalypse

Some stuff got destroyed,
And the world descended into a lake of fire.
Where is everybody?

ACKNOWLEDGEMENTS

One thousand thank yous to: Devin Aubrey Roth, for constant wit, wisdom, and brilliance. Samuel Keck Scott, for the old times and the new beginnings. David Scott, for inspiration, sincerity, and honesty. Hilary Bozley Marea Barnard, for plain old downhome friendship, laughter, and the appreciation of awkwardness. Michelle Frances Krezanoski, for being a good spiritual other. Lisa Chakmak, for intensity and knowing. Dustin Skylar Tassencourt Wright, for being willing to imagine. Logan Jensen, for long conversations about creative things. Willow Sofie Samaya Abel, for being a catalyst. John Johnson, for teaching me how to work out at the gym, and for breakfast. Creatch Rose Moss-Maguire, for Wednesdays. Carebear Tillman Chase, for music. Felicity Elizabeth Palma, the biggest jerk I have ever known. Kaytee Green Fink, for brightness. Judith Aviva Mayer, for sex, history, and laughing. Zeya Schindler, for point of view. Lexi Daly, for matters of the ethereal, and the heart. Will Scott, for bringing people together. Molly Greene, for your great big grin. Kate Deluna Cadoux, for letting me sit on her lap while I was puking in the desert when she barely knew me. Sofia Rose Smith, for insight and magic and twilight. Lauren Shomaker, for being young, crazy and in love with me when I was 18 years old and stupid. Ariella Daly, for playing the piano. Lisa Piazza, Judith Klinger, and Chris Carmen, the teachers who meant something. Adam and Gif at The Crepe Place. Wes Anthony and the E-3 Playhouse. Richard Stockton and the Planet Cruz Comedy Hour. Joe and Caitlyn at the Firefly. Irene Hammaker and the Cowell Fireside Lounge. Melody Rose Thomson Stone, for loving, and teaching, me. Zoe Ruiz, for invaluable help and advice with this book. Deb Bevilacqua, for her imagination and her help. Elliott Austin Kuhn, you are a goddamn warrior in every sense of the word, my friend, thank you. Norris Howard Buckman, this book would not exist, if you didn't. Erin Emily Bailey Boyle, for being the one I grew up with (sorry if I was a jerk sometimes). Pamela Sue Bailey Boyle and Daniel Leo Boyle, for endless and undying support and love, and you know...my existence (thank you, thank you, thank you). Kellee English, in all possible worlds, I am the luckiest man that exists, and you are the reason why.

Ok, if this was the oscars they would have started playing music to make me stop a long time ago. I could go on forever. All you other people that I love and have loved, I hope you know it.

ABOUT THE AUTHOR: Shimmy Boyle likes cartoons. And ducks. If he ever shakes your hand, he hopes his handshake is as firm as his mother taught him it should be. He loves listening to cities hum in the middle of the night. He believes in ghosts, and the moon. His favorite place is the woods. When he was a child, Shimmy was obsessed with the concept of magic words, the idea of a phrase which by simply speaking it aloud would cause something miraculous to happen: a rabbit to appear out of a hat, the opening of a secret door into a chamber filled with treasure, or best of all, give him the ability to breathe underwater. It would be safe to say that his becoming a writer was the result of his search for the right combination of magic words.

He is still looking for them.

www.shimmypoetry.com

thank you.

Made in the USA
Monee, IL
07 July 2026

56551366R10080